Practise
Algebra
KS3
Age 11–14
Hilary Koll and Steve Mills

Contents

Introduction	2
Simplifying expressions	3
Collecting like terms	5
Adding and subtracting letters	7
Constants and variables	9
Substitution	11
Expanding brackets and factorising	13
Activity cards	15
Solving simple equations	19
Solving equations by balancing	21
Solving equations using inverses	23
Solving more complex equations	25
Letters on both sides of an equation	27
Formulae	29
Answers	31

Introduction

Practise Algebra

Practise Algebra is for anyone who is struggling to understand concepts in algebra like expressions and equations, and all the other difficult ideas usually covered in maths lessons at Key Stage 3. Algebra is a topic that most people find difficult at first, but this simple, step-by-step approach should have you simplifying, factorising expressions and solving equations in no time.

Part 1 (pages 3–14) of this book is all about expressions, including simplifying expressions, expanding brackets, factorising, and substituting. Part 2 (pages 19–30) deals with equations and formulae, including solving equations using two different methods (you can choose the method you prefer). Also covered are using formulae and changing the subject of them.

How to use *Practise*

Work through each section in order, reading all the clues and tips in the margins as you go through the exercises. You will need to cut out the cards in the centre of the book to use for some activities. Make sure you keep these cards in a safe place, such as an envelope, so you can re-use them.

When you feel confident with what is written on a particular page, turn over and try to answer the questions on the next page. Carefully mark all your answers and see how you got on. If you still have any difficulties and feel you need some more practice, try some of the activities again or re-read the tips and comments in the margins. If you feel confident and have got most of the questions right, move on to the next section.

You might find it helpful to make a list of all the key words that you come across in this book and write down the meanings. This will help you when you try to answer the questions.

First published in 2007
exclusively for WHSmith by
Hodder Education, part of Hachette Livre UK,
338 Euston Road
London NW1 3BH

Impression number   10 9 8 7 6 5 4 3 2
Year   2010 2009 2008
Text and illustrations © Hodder Murray 2007

All rights reserved. Apart from any use permitted under UK copyright law, no part of this publication may be reproduced or transmitted in any form or by any means, electronic or mechanical, including photocopying, recording, or any information storage and retrieval system, without permission in writing from the publisher or under licence from the Copyright Licensing Agency Limited. Further details of such licences (for reprographic reproduction) may be obtained from the Copyright Licensing Agency Limited, Saffron House, 6–10 Kirby Street, London EC1N 8TS

Text: Hilary Koll and Steve Mills (e-mail: info@cmeprojects.com)
Cover illustration by Sally Newton Illustrations
Typeset by Fakenham Photosetting Limited, Fakenham, Norfolk
Printed and bound in Spain

A CIP record for this book is available from the British Library

ISBN 978 0 340 94288 8

Simplifying expressions

Practice

In algebra, letters are used to stand for numbers.

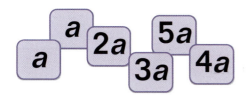

- Cut out the 'a' cards on page 15.
- Turn them face down and pick *three* of them.
- Write them like this:

  a + 2a + a   4a

  a + 2a + a is called an **expression**.

- Now find out how many *a*'s there are altogether.

  a + 2a + a = 4a   =

  (4a means '4 lots of *a*')

- This process is called **simplifying**.
  (Writing the expression in a simpler, shorter way.)

Confusing times?

In algebra, it could be easy to confuse the multiplication sign with the letter x, so when writing 4 × *a*, leave out the × sign and just write **4a** (4 lots of *a*).

If a number and any letters are next to each other, they are multiplied together, e.g. **2ab** means 2 × *a* × *b*.

Word wise

When letters or numbers are written without an equals sign, such as *a* + 2, this is called an **expression**.
Part 2 of this book looks at **equations**. Equations always have an equals sign.

Try it

Pick three cards and simplify the expression.

a + 2a + 3a = 6a

Do this several times to get the hang of it.
Then try picking more than three cards.

- Remember this word:

  simplifying – writing an expression more simply

Clues and tips

An **expression** can be written in many different ways and still be worth the same, such as:

$a + a + a$
or $a + 2a$
or $2a + a$
or $3a$
or $3 \times a$
or $a \times 3$

Which expressions in question 1 are **equivalent** (worth the same)?

Watch out

It is easy to forget to write the letter *a* in the answer.

The letter doesn't matter

Treat question 3 in the same way as question 1.

It does not matter what the letter is.

What next?

If you are fine with this topic, go on to page 5.

If not, practise more with your 'a' cards.

Try it yourself!

1. **Simplify** these.

   $a + 3a + a =$ __5a__ $a + a + a + a + 2a =$ __6a__

   $a + a + 2a + a =$ __5a__ $3a + a + 2a + a + a =$ __8a__

   $2a + 3a + 2a =$ __7a__ $3a + a + a + a + 5a =$ __11a__

   $a + 5a + 5a + a =$ __12a__ $6a + 4a + 2a + a + 2a =$ __15a__

2. **True or false?** Have these expressions been correctly **simplified**?

   $a + a + a = 3a$ __true__ $a + 3a + a + 3a = 8a$ __true__

   $7a + a + 3a = 11a$ __true__ $5a + a + 3a + a = 9a$ __false__

   $3a + 3a = 9a$ __False__ $6a + 3a + a + 4a = 14$ __false__

   $a + 5a + a = 7a$ __true__ $4a + 4a + 2a + a + 2a = 13a$ __true__

   $a + 6a + 2a = 9$ __true__ $10a + 10a + 5a + 5a = 25a$ __false__

3. **Simplify** these – notice that different letters are used.

   $m + 3m + m =$ __5m__ $g + g + 2g + g + 3g =$ __8g__

   $p + p + 2p + 3p =$ __7p__ $3s + s + s + s + s =$ __7s__

   $2c + 3c + 4c =$ __9c__ $9d + d + d + d + 4d =$ __16d__

   $y + 5y + 5y + 2y =$ __13y__ $7k + 3k + 2k + k + 2k =$ __15k__

Collecting like terms

Practice

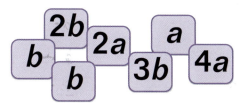

- Now cut out the '*b*' cards on page 15.
- Shuffle them with the '*a*' cards.
- Pick four cards. (Hopefully, some will be '*a*' cards and some will be '*b*' cards.)

- Write them out like this:

  $a + 2b + b + 4a$

- To **simplify** these expressions, find out *how many a's* there are and then *how many b's* there are and write this down.

  $a + 2b + b + 4a = 5a + 3b$ (Notice that the *a*'s do not mix with the *b*'s.)

  Now try simplifying your expression!

  _____

- This process is called **collecting like terms**.

Try it

Pick four cards and simplify the **expression** by collecting like terms.

$$b + 2a + 4b + a = 3a + 5b$$

Do this several times to get the hang of it.
Then try picking more than four cards.
- Remember this:
  collecting like terms – grouping letters that are the same

Why is algebra needed?

Algebra is used in all sorts of situations, such as helping companies to make more profit, helping engineers build roads and bridges, or even helping doctors to decide how much of a drug to give a person.

In each of these situations, there are usually one or more unknown values that need to be calculated from a number of known values.

Watch out

$3a + 5b$ could also be written as $5b + 3a$. They are both the same. It does not matter in which order you put the letters.

Clues and tips

The reason different letters are used in an expression is that they could stand for different numbers.

Here are some number cards showing the numbers 2 and 5.

a is written on the back of the number 2 cards and b is written on the back of the number 5 cards. So $3a + 4b$ is made using 3 cards with 2 on and 4 cards with 5 on, giving a total of 26.

More than two letters

It does not matter how many letters there are – just do not mix them.

It can help to cross letters off as they are counted.

What next?

If you are fine with this topic, go on to page 7.

If not, practise more with your 'a' and 'b' cards.

Try it yourself!

1. **Simplify** these by **collecting like terms**.

   $a + 3a + 2b + 4b =$ __4a + 6b__ $a + b + a + b + 2a =$ _4a+2b_

   $a + b + 2b + a =$ _2a+3b_ $3b + b + 2b + a + a =$ _2a+6b_

   $2a + 3b + 2a =$ _4a+3b_ $6a + b + b + b + 2a =$ _8a+3b_

2. Which of these expressions, when **simplified**, has the answer $4a + 3b$? Tick them.

   $a + 3a + 2b + b =$ __4a + 3b__ ✓ $a + 2b + a + b + 2a =$ _4a+3b_

   $a + b + 3a + 2a =$ _6a+1b_ $3a + b + 2b + a =$ _4a+3b_ ✓

   $4a + b + 2b =$ _4a+3b_ ✓ $a + a + 3b + a + a =$ _4a+3b_ ✓

3. **Collect like terms** – notice that different letters are used.

   $g + 3g + h + h =$ __4g + 2h__ $m + m + 2n + n + 3m =$ _5m+3n_

   $2c + 3d + c + 4c =$ _7c+3d_ $9e + f + f + f + 4e =$ _13e+3f_

   $x + 5y + 5x + 2y =$ _6x+7y_ $7j + 3k + 2j + k + 2k =$ _9j+6k_

4. **Collect like terms** – with *more than two* different letters.

   $a + 3a + b + c + 2b + 3c + a + 4a =$ _____9a + 3b + 4c_____

   $2p + 5q + q + r + 2r + p + p + 3q =$ _9q+3r+4p_

   $x + 4x + 2y + 3z + 2y + 5z + 6x + 4y =$ _11x+8y+8z_

Adding and subtracting letters

Practice

So far, letters have just been added together. They can be subtracted, too.

- Use all the cut-out 'a' cards.
- Place the 5a card face up on the table.
- Turn the others face down.
- Pick a card and *subtract* that amount from 5a.
- Write it like shown below and work out the answer. Do this twice.

$5a - a = 4a$ $5a - \underline{}$ $5a - \underline{}$

This is still **simplifying** an **expression**.

- Now also use the cut-out 'b' cards.
- Place the 5b card next to the 5a card.
- Write this as 5a + 5b.
- Turn the rest face down and mix them with the others.
- Pick a card and *subtract* that amount from 5a + 5b.
- Write it like this and remember to keep the letters separate:

$5a + 5b - \underline{\;a\;} = 4a + 5b$ Only subtract a from $5a$,
$5a + 5b - \underline{} = \underline{}$ the 5b stays the same.

Fancy a take-away?

Letters can only be subtracted from things of the same type, for example 5a subtract 4b can only be written as $5a - 4b$. This is because a's and b's are not the same.

5a subtract 4a can be written more simply because they are both a's. It can be written as just a.

Try it

Pick a card and subtract it from 5a + 5b.

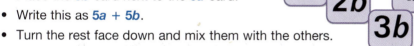

Do this several times to get the hang of it.

Try picking two cards to subtract.

- Answers sometimes contain negatives, like this:

$5a + 5b - 4a - 3a = -2a + 5b$
$5a + 5b - 4b - 2b = 5a + -b$ or $5a - b$

Watch out

Looking at just the a's, it can be seen that $5a - 4a - 3a$ gives $-2a$ (negative 2a). The 5b stays the same.

If an add sign and a negative sign appear next to each other, this is written as a subtraction sign.

Clues and tips

It is important to look very carefully to see whether each part is added or subtracted to avoid getting the completely wrong answer.

Do not forget that $1b$ is written as just b.

Take it one step at a time

When simplifying the expressions in question 2, take the letter a first and go through each part of the expression. It can help to *cross letters off* or *underline* them as they are counted. Then move on to the letter b.

Negative issues

Do not panic if there are a negative number of a's or b's. Just write the negative sign in the answer.

What next?

If you are fine with this topic, go on to page 9. If you find the negative ones difficult, draw a number line from −10 to 10 to help you.

Try it yourself!

1. **Simplify** these.

   $5a - a =$ *4a* $6a - 2a =$ *4a*

   $8a - a - a =$ *6a* $5a + 5b - 2a =$ *3a + 5b*

   $5a + 5b - a - 2a =$ *2a + 5b* $5a + 5b - a - b =$ *4a + 4b*

   $5a + 5b - 4b =$ *[scribbled]* $7a + 4b - 4a - 3a =$ *4b*

   $3a + 10b - 4b =$ *[scribbled]* $7a + 3b - 2b - a =$ *6a + 1b*

   $5a + 2b - b - 4a =$ *[scribbled]* $8a + 4b - 4b - a - a =$ *6a*

2. These are even harder to **simplify**. Can you do it?

   $10a + 10b - 4a - a - b - a - a - 2b =$ *3a + 7b*

   $10a + 10b - 2a - 2a - 3b - a - b - b =$ *5a + 5b*

   $12a + 8b - 2a - 5a - 4b - a - b - a =$ *3a + 3b*

   $7a + 11b - 2b - 5b - 4b - a - 2a - a =$ *3a + 0b*

3. **Simplify** these – the answers might be negative.

   $2a + 4b - 6b =$ *2a − 2b*

   $4a + 2b - 8b =$ *−6b + 4a*

   $2a + 3b - 3a =$ *−a + 3b*

   $3a + 6b - 6a =$ *−3a + 6b*

   $2a + 4b - 3a - b =$ *−a + 3b*

   $4a + 3b - 8b - 3a =$ *+a − 5b*

Constants and variables

Practice

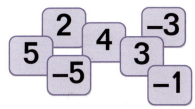

- Now cut out the number cards on page 17. Any number on its own (not one next to a letter) is called a **constant**. This is because a number, unlike letters, is always *constant*; it stays the same. Constants can be positive or negative.
- Letters in **expressions** are known as **variables**. This is because, in an expression, the value of a letter can *vary*. For example, in the expression **2y**, y could stand for 3, 7, -10 or any number.
- Shuffle the constant cards with the variable cards ('a' and 'b' cards).
- Pick five cards. (Hopefully, some will be variables and some will be constants.)
- Write them out like this, adding them all together:

  $a + 2b + b + 4 + -1$ If an add sign and a negative sign appear next to each other, they are written as a subtraction sign.
  $a + 2b + b + 4 - 1$

- To **simplify** these expressions, find out *how many a's* there are and *how many b's* there are, and then add the constants together.

  $a + 2b + b + 4 - 1 = a + 3b + 3$

  Now try with your expression.

  _____

Where did the word 'algebra' come from?

An Arabic mathematician called al-Khwarizmi first used the word 'algebra' over 1000 years ago.

Don't mix them

Notice that the a's do not mix with the b's and that the **variables** are kept separate from the **constants**.

Again, it does not matter in which order the parts are given so, $a + 3b + 3$ could be written as $3 + a + 3b$, etc. Generally, however, most people put variables first and constants at the end.

Try it

Pick several cards, add them together and simplify the expression by **collecting like terms**.

$$\boxed{b} + \boxed{2a} + \boxed{4b} + \boxed{-2} = 2a + 5b - 2$$

How many cards can you simplify?

Clues and tips
If an add sign and a negative sign appear next to each other, they are written just as a subtraction sign.

Watch out
Look very carefully at each part of question 2 to see if it is being *added to* or *subtracted from* the other parts.

Use a number line
If you find it difficult to add and subtract numbers with negative answers, draw a number line from −10 to 10.

Count backwards when **subtracting positive numbers** or **adding negative numbers**.

What next?
Make up more questions using the 'a' and 'b' cards and the positive constants. (Remove the negative numbers for this.) Use the addition and subtraction signs on page 17.

Try it yourself!

1. **Simplify these by collecting like terms.**

    $4a + 5b + 2a + 2b + 3b + 6 + 4 + -3 =$ ___$6a + 10b + 7$___

    Think of this part as $6 + 4 - 3$

    $2a + 6b + 2a + 5a + 4b + b + 5 + -2 =$ ___$9a + 11b + 7$___

    $7a + 4b + 2b + 5 + 2a + 3 + 2a + -10 =$ ___$11a + 6b + 8$___

    $4a + b + 5b + -4 + 3a + 5 + 2b + 2 =$ ___$7a + 7b + 11$___

    $10 + 2a + 5 + -5 + 3b + 5a + b + -1 =$ ___$7a + 4b + 21$___

2. **Try simplifying these expressions, but notice that some of the parts are *subtracted* rather than *added*.**

    $7a + 4b - 2a + 5b - 2b + 9 + 1 - 4 =$ _____

    $3a + 5b - 3b - 2a + 5b + 4 - 5 + 2 =$ _____

    $6a + 3b + 5a - 4a - 3b + 6 + 1 - 10 =$ _____

    $-2a + 4b + 5a - 2b + 8 - 3 - 9 =$ _____

3. **Simplify these – notice that different letters are used.**

    $3c + 5d - 3c - 2d + 2c + 6 - 5 + 3 =$ _____

    $6m + 3n + 5m + 6 - 4n - 3m + 1 - 4 =$ _____

    $-2g + 3h + 5g + 10 - 2h - 3 - 7 =$ _____

    $3s - t + 4 + 5s - 6 + 2 + 11t - 7s =$ _____

Substitution

Practice

- Now you are going to learn how to **substitute**.
- You will need just your 'a' cards again. Turn them face down.

Imagine you are about to win lots of money.

If you pick this card [a] you win an amount of money.

If you pick this card [2a] you win twice the amount.

If you pick this card [3a] you win three times the amount and so on.

- Pick one of your 'a' cards.
  How much money would you win?
  Until someone tells you what 'a' is worth you do not know!
  How much would you win if a is worth **£5**?
  What if a is worth **£10**?
  Or if $a =$ **£1000**?

- This is called **substituting**.
  Like footballers who get substituted (put in place of another player), here a **number** is put in place of a **letter**.

- Find these two cards:

- Substitute the following values for a and b to find how much money you would win:

  If $a =$ £5 and $b =$ £2   3 lots of £5 + 4 lots of £2 = £15 + £8 = £23

  If $a =$ £3 and $b =$ £5   _____

  If $a =$ £10 and $b =$ £6   _____

  If $a =$ £6 and $b =$ £1   _____

Word wise

To **substitute** means 'to exchange one thing for another'. In sport, players are substituted. When solving problems in algebra, numbers are substituted for letters.

One of the most useful parts of algebra for everyday life is being able to substitute a number into an expression or formula. Find out more about formulae on page 29.

Remember this

Do not forget that $3a$ means '3 lots of a' or '$3 \times a$'.

When substituting a value for a into the expression $3a$, it must be multiplied by 3, like this:

If $a = 5$, then $3a = 15$.

Clues and tips

Substitute = swap so in question 1, part 4:
If *k* is 11, then
6*k* is 6 × 11 = 66
so
6*k* + 1 is 66 + 1 = 67

Substituting two letters

Here are some number cards showing the numbers 2 and 5.

a is written on the back of the number 2 cards and *b* is written on the back of the number 5 cards. So 3*a* + 2*b* is made using three cards with 2 on and two cards with 5 on, giving a total of 16.

What next?

Watch out for whether to add or subtract each part of the expression. Sometimes, wrong answers are due to adding rather than subtracting.

For more substituting see page 19.

Try it yourself!

1. **Substitute** the number given for the letter in these expressions.

   If $a = 4$, find the value of $5a$ $5a = 20$

   If $y = 2$, find the value of $7y$ _____

   If $d = 5$, find the value of $8d$ _____

   If $k = 11$, find the value of $6k + 1$ $6k + 1 = 67$

   If $x = 10$, find the value of $9x + 5$ _____

   If $g = 3$, find the value of $5g + 4$ _____

   If $q = 1$, find the value of $10q - 2$ _____

2. **Substitute** the numbers for the letters to find the value of each expression.

   If $a = 4$ and $b = 2$, find the value of $5a + 3b$ $20 + 6 = 26$

   If $a = 2$ and $b = 5$, find the value of $3a + 2b$ _____

   If $a = 9$ and $b = 1$, find the value of $a + 4b$ _____

   If $a = 3$ and $b = 6$, find the value of $2a + 2b$ _____

3. If $x = 6$ and $y = 9$, find the values of each expression.

   $x + 5y - 1$ _____ $3x + 2y + 5$ _____

   $2x + 2y - 5$ _____ $5x - y + 3$ _____

   $3x + 10y - 8$ _____ $7x - 3y + 14$ _____

   $6x + 7y - 11$ _____ $-2x + 4y - 6$ _____

Expanding brackets and factorising

Practice

- Here are some expressions:

  | $a + b$ | $c + 3$ | $2d - 5$ | $6e - f + 2$ |

- Look what happens when each expression is **multiplied** by a **constant**.

  | $4(a + b)$ | $5(c + 3)$ | $2(2d - 5)$ | $3(6e - f + 2)$ |

  Notice that they all have **brackets**. Brackets show that what is outside the bracket is multiplied by everything inside.

- Expressions *with* brackets can also be written *without* brackets. To do so, multiply the number outside the bracket by **each part** inside.

  $4(a + b) \rightarrow 4a + 4b$
  $5(c + 3) \rightarrow 5c + 15$
  $2(2d - 5) \rightarrow 4d - 10$
  $3(6e - f + 2) \rightarrow 18e - 3f + 6$

  This is called **expanding the brackets**. It is a type of simplifying.

  The opposite of expanding is called **factorising**. Factorising means finding a **factor** that divides into each part of an expression.

  $18e - 3f + 6$ —**Factorising**→ $3(6e - f + 2)$

  3 is a factor of **each part**

- Remember:
  - **expanding** – multiplying what is outside the brackets by each part inside. **(Getting rid of the brackets.)**
  - **factorising** – finding a factor that divides into each part and putting it outside brackets. **(Putting back the brackets.)**

Remember this
A number on its own (not next to a letter) is called a **constant**. It can be positive or negative.

Multiplying by variables
A simple expression can also be multiplied by a **variable**, like the letter x or y, to create an expression such as $x(x + 2)$.

Draw arrows
When expanding brackets, it helps to draw arrows to remind you to multiply the part outside by *every part* inside.

Factorising facts
A **factor** is a number or a variable that divides exactly into another number.

When **factorising**, take this factor outside and put brackets around the rest of the expression.

Clues and tips

The most common mistake in expanding brackets is to forget to multiply what is outside the brackets by *every part* inside.

When expanding

$5(a + b)$

the answer is NOT

$5a + b$

the answer is

$5a + 5b$

Example

Look at this example for multiplying several letters by a number:

If multiplying $3a$ by 5, remember that $3a$ means '3 lots of a'.

Multiplying that by 5, gives 15 lots of a which is $15a$.

What next?

Do you feel that you understand the ideas in the book so far? Now is a good time to look back and go over the pages to check that you still understand.

Try it yourself!

1. **Simplify** these expressions by **expanding the brackets.**

   $2(a + b) =$ __2a + 2b__ $4(y - 2) =$ __4y - 8__

   $5(c + 2) =$ _____ $3(k + 6) =$ _____

   $6(m + n) =$ _____ $7(2a - 1) =$ _____

   $4(5g + h) =$ _____ $6(2f - e) =$ _____

   $8(10s + 3t) =$ _____ $5(3y - 7) =$ _____

   $3(a + 3b - 2) =$ _____ $2(m + 7n + 4) =$ _____

   $5(4c + d - 3e) =$ _____ $6(g - 2h - 5) =$ _____

2. **Factorise** these expressions by putting brackets in. Check each of your answers by **expanding the brackets.**

   $2a + 2b =$ __2(a+b)__ $2c - 4 =$ __2(c-2)__

   $5d + 10 =$ _____ $3k + 6 =$ _____

   $6m + 4n =$ _____ $2a - 12 =$ _____

   $10g + 20h =$ _____ $6f - 2e =$ _____

   $15s + 3t =$ _____ $5y - 25 =$ _____

   $2a + 4b - 6 =$ __2(a + 2b - 3)__ $2m + 6n + 4 =$ _____

   $15c + 5d - 10e =$ _____ $8g - 4h - 12 =$ _____

Activity cards

'a' cards

a	3a
a	4a
2a	4a
2a	5a
3a	5a

'b' cards

b	3b
b	4b
2b	4b
2b	5b
3b	5b

Activity cards

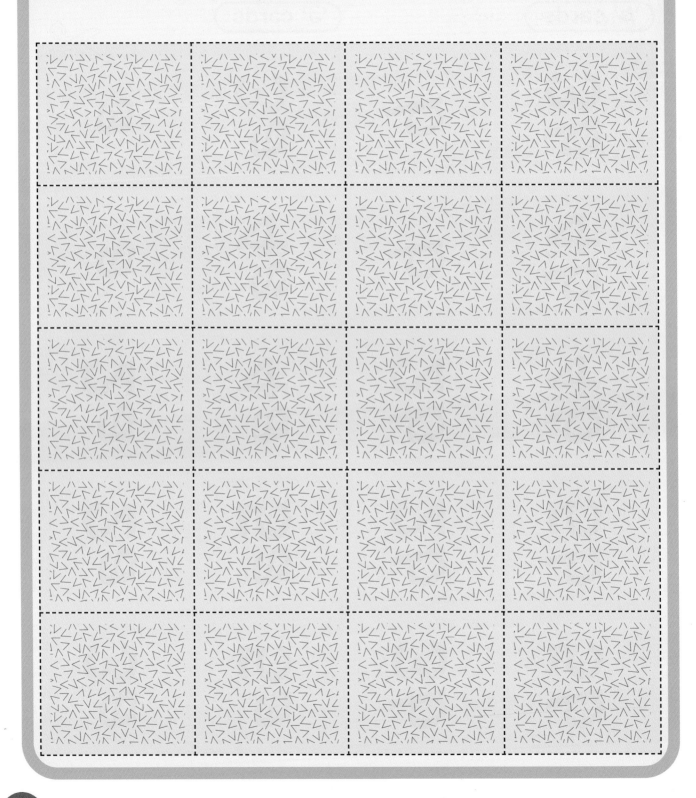

Activity cards

Addition, subtraction and equals signs

Constant cards

+		-1	1
+		-2	2
+		-3	3
+		-4	4
=	=	-5	5

Activity cards

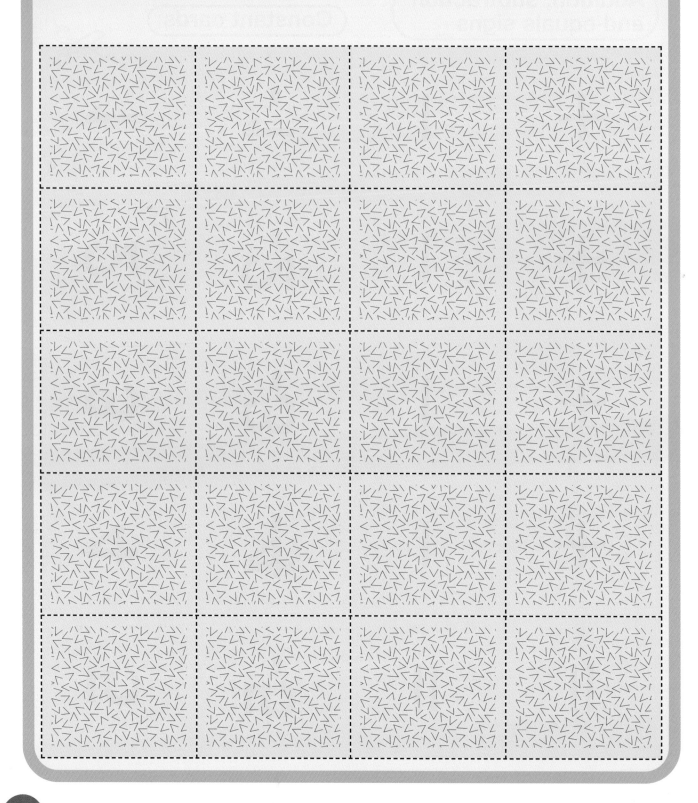

Solving simple equations

Practice

- Part 2 of this book is going to look at **equations**.
- An equation always has an equals sign. What is on one side of the equals sign is worth the same as what is on the other side.

  Like:

  $2a = 6$ or $2y + 3 = 4y - 1$

  $2a$ is worth the same as **6** $2y + 3$ is worth the same as $4y - 1$

- If only one letter is used in an equation, it is possible to **solve the equation**.

  Solving the equation means finding out what number the letter stands for. It is like cracking a code.

- Look at each of the following equations. Imagine that a number is hidden underneath each letter. What number would this be to make each number sentence correct?

  $a + 4 = 10$ $b - 2 = 7$ $5 \times c = 15$

  a must be 6   *b* must be 9   *c* must be 3

  This is called solving the equation.

- Use the cut-out cards to make each of these equations. Solve each of them.

  $a + 3 = 5$ $6 - b = 1$

  $2a = 4$ $2b = 6$ $3a = 12$

- Check your solutions by **substituting** the number for the letter on one side to see if it equals what is on the other side.
- Remember this:

  solving the equation – finding out what number a letter stands for in an equation

Puzzles

Being able to solve equations can help us with all kinds of problems and puzzles.

Look at this puzzle:

I think of a number and add 5 to it. The answer is 14. What is my number?

Let us call the number *n* (or any other letter we choose).

This puzzle can be written as $n + 5 = 14$

It can help us to see that $n = 9$

Watch out

Remember that $5 \times c$ is usually written as $5c$ in algebra.

Crack the code

To solve the equation (crack the code), imagine what number must be hidden beneath each letter to make the number sentence true.

For more on **substituting** see page 11.

Clues and tips

To **substitute**, put the answer back into the equation:

$a + 7 = 10$

so the answer is

$a = 3$.

Check by putting 3 in place of a. This gives $3 + 7 = 10$.

If this number sentence is true then you know the answer is correct.

Division difficulties

Division questions in algebra are not usually written with a division sign (÷). Instead, they are written as one number beneath another like a fraction.

$p ÷ 2$ could be written as $\frac{p}{2}$

What next?

Some people find it really easy to see the solutions to equations, but other people prefer to use another method. If you are one of them, check out the next four pages. You might find it easier to use one of the methods there.

Try it yourself!

1. **Solve these equations** and check your solutions by substituting.

   $a + 7 = 10$ __a = 3__ $b - 5 = 3$ _____

   $12 + c = 20$ _____ $22 - d = 19$ _____

   $10 = e + 8$ _____ $13 = f - 5$ _____

   $2g = 20$ __g = 10__ $3h = 15$ _____

   $10 = 5j$ _____ $6k = 24$ _____

   $66 = 11m$ _____ $7n = 49$ _____

2. Write these puzzles as **equations** and **solve** them.

   I think of a number and add 6 to it. The answer is 23.

   _____$n + 6 = 23$ so $n = 17$_____

   I think of a number and subtract 11 from it. The answer is 44.

   _____

   I think of a number and subtract it from 27. The answer is 18.

   _____

   I think of a number and multiply it by 5. The answer is 40.

   _____

3. **Solve** these **equations** that involve division.

   $p ÷ 2 = 10$ _____ $q ÷ 4 = 5$ _____

   $27 ÷ r = 3$ _____ $45 ÷ s = 9$ _____

   $t ÷ 4 = 10$ _____ $u ÷ 6 = 8$ _____

Solving equations by balancing

Practice

- Sometimes it is not easy to spot the solution to an **equation**.
- There are two different ways of solving these. This page looks at a method of **solving equations** using ideas of **balancing**.
  Both sides of an equation are worth the same – they balance.

$$2y + 3 = 11$$

$2y + 3$ is worth the same as 11
$2y + 3$ and 11 balance

THE RULES

- Whatever is done to one side of an equation, must be done to the other so that both sides still balance.
- You can add, subtract, multiply or divide one side of an equation – but you must do the same to the other side, too.
- Aim to get the **letter** on its own **on one side** and the numbers on the other side.
- To get rid of something from one side, do the opposite. If it is an **add** then **subtract**, if it is a **times** then **divide** and vice versa.

Remember this
Remember that when adding and subtracting parts of an expression (see page 7), you can only add or subtract a **number** from a **number** or a **letter** from the same **letter**.
Like this . . .

$$2a + 5 - 2$$
$$= 2a + 3$$
$$4b - 8 + 8$$

Watch out
Here, because numbers are being added and subtracted, the letters do not change.

$$2y + 3 = 11$$

a) -3 -3
     $2y$ $=$ 8

b) $\div 2$ $\div 2$
     y $=$ 4

a) Get rid of the **+3** on the left. (Do the opposite by subtracting 3 and do the same to both sides.)

b) Get rid of the **× 2** on the left. (Do the opposite by dividing by 2, and do the same to both sides.)

Watch out
$2y$ is the same as $y \times 2$, so to get just y we **divide** both sides by **2**.

- This has **solved the equation**. The solution is **y = 4**.
- Check the **solution** by **substituting** the number for the letter on one side to see if it equals what is on the other side.

$$2y + 3 = 11$$

$y = 4$ so $2 \times 4 + 3$ should equal 11.
$8 + 3$ *does* equal 11, so the solution $y = 4$ is correct.

Remember this
'Solution' is just another word for 'answer'.
For more on **substituting** see page 11.

Clues and tips

Remember to follow the rules of solving equations by balancing (see page 21).

Help for $4c - 5 = 27$

Try to get c on its own.

First get rid of the -5.

(Do the opposite: **add** 5 to both sides.)

Then, to get just c on its own remember to **divide** by 4.

The other way round

Do not worry that the equations in question 2 are the other way around. Just treat them in the same way.

For the first one, try to get f on its own (on the right-hand side this time). Start by getting rid of the $+12$. Then just follow the rules.

What next?

There are two main ways of solving equations. If you find this way too hard, you might prefer the way shown on the next two pages.

Try it yourself!

1. **Solve these equations using ideas of balancing.**

   $5b - 7 = 43$

   $$\begin{array}{rcl} & +7 & +7 \\ 5b & = & 50 \\ \div 5 & & \div 5 \\ b & = & 10 \end{array}$$

   $4c - 5 = 27$

   _____

   $6d + 9 = 51$

   $3e + 8 = 26$

   _____   _____

2. **Solve these equations in the same way.**

   $34 = 2f + 12$

   $19 = 6g - 5$

   _____   _____

   $42 = 9h - 3$

   $27 = 7k + 6$

   _____   _____

   Remember to check all solutions by **substituting**.

Solving equations using inverses

Practice

- Some people prefer this way to **solve equations**.
- To use this method needs an understanding of **inverses**.
  Every operation has an inverse (or opposite).

The inverse of addition is subtraction	+	−
The inverse of subtraction is addition	−	+
The inverse of multiplication is division	×	÷
The inverse of division is multiplication	÷	×

- The idea of this method is to work backwards, using inverses. Think of this equation as a trail of instructions, *starting with the letter*.

$$2y + 3 = 11$$

   Start with y → multiply it by 2 → then add 3 → to get to 11

Now write this backwards, starting at 11.

   to get to y ← divide by 2 ← subtract 3 ← Start with 11

Notice that the inverse has been used for each operation and that the order is reversed.
These new instructions could be written as ...

$$(11 - 3) \div 2 = y$$ ... and then find y.

$$(11 - 3) \div 2 = y$$
$$8 \div 2 = y$$
$$4 = y$$ so y must equal 4.

- This has **solved the equation**. The solution is $y = 4$.

- As always, check the solution by **substituting** the number for the letter on one side to see if it equals what is on the other side.

$$2y + 3 = 11$$

$y = 4$ so $2 \times 4 + 3$ should equal 11.
$8 + 3$ *does* equal 11, so the solution $y = 4$ is correct.

BODMAS

Have you ever heard of the word BODMAS?

This is a way of helping you remember the order in which calculations are carried out.

Brackets (Do anything in brackets first)
Other (Do other things, including squaring or finding the square root)
Divide (Then divide or
Multiply multiply numbers)
Add (Finally add or
Subtract subtract numbers)

Watch out

Notice that $11 - 3$ is put in brackets to show that it must be worked out first.

For more on **substituting** see page 11.

Clues and tips

Do not forget that 5*b* means

'5 multiplied by *b*'

or

'*b* multiplied by 5'.

In the same way, 4*c* means

'4 multiplied by *c*'

or

'*c* multiplied by 4'.

Always check the solution by substituting

There should be no need to look at the answers in the back. You should know whether the solution is right or wrong. See page 23 for a reminder of how to check.

What next?

Look back over the last four pages. Do you prefer the balancing method or the inverse method? It does not matter which method you use as long as you can get to the right answer every time.

Try it yourself!

1. **Solve** these **equations** using **inverses**.

$$5b - 7 = 43$$

Start with *b* → multiply by 5 → subtract 7 → to get to 43

to get to *b* ← divide by 5 ← add 7 ← Start with 43

$(43 + 7) \div 5 = b$

$50 \div 5 = b$

$10 = b$ or $b = 10$

$$4c - 5 = 27$$

Start with *c* →

$$6d + 9 = 51$$

2. **Solve** these **equations**. Do your working out *on paper*.

$5e + 8 = 33$ $36 = 3f + 12$ $30 = 8g - 10$

$32 = 7h - 3$ $31 = 2j + 13$ $38 = 5k - 17$

$24 = 5m - 6$ $65 = 7n + 16$ $57 = 8p - 7$

Remember to check all solutions by **substituting**.

Solving more complex equations

Practice

- Some equations are harder as they may include **brackets**.
- If an equation has brackets, it is usually easier to **expand** them first and then **solve** the equation as before.

$$4(y + 3) = 54 \qquad 4y + 12 = 54$$

- Once the equation is without brackets, solve it using **balancing** or **inverses** – whichever you prefer.

- Sometimes, when solving equations, the solution might be a **decimal** rather than a whole number. Look at the method you prefer. Notice how below, 42 is divided by 4.
A calculator could be used to find the solution.

balancing

$$4y + 12 = 54$$

	-12		-12
$4y$		$=$	42
$\div 4$			$\div 4$
y		$=$	10.5

- As always, check the solution by **substituting** the number for the letter on one side to see if it equals what is on the other side.

$$4y + 12 = 54$$

$y = 10.5$ so $4 \times 10.5 + 12$ should equal 54.
$42 + 12$ *does* equal 54, so $y = 10.5$ is correct.

inverses

$$4y + 12 = 54$$

Start with $y \rightarrow$ multiply by 4 $\rightarrow$ add 12 $\rightarrow$ to get to 54
to get to $y \leftarrow$ divide by 4 $\leftarrow$ subtract 12 $\leftarrow$ Start with 54

$(54 - 12) \div 4 = y$
$\qquad 42 \div 4 = y$
$\qquad\quad$ so $y = 10.5$

Clues and tips
Remind yourself about how to **expand brackets** by looking again at pages 13 and 14.

Solving equations with brackets
It *is* possible to solve equations *without* expanding the brackets. Your teacher might have taught this method. It does not matter which method is used as long as the correct answer is reached each time.

Decimal difficulties
Use a calculator to divide the numbers. If the decimal has many digits after the decimal point, like 4.5725163485, then just round it to 2 **decimal places** (so that the answer has 2 digits after the decimal point).

Clues and tips

When expanding brackets, it helps to draw arrows as a reminder to multiply the part outside by *every part* inside.

In question 2, round the answer if it is a decimal with lots of digits after the decimal point, e.g. 3.583625167 can be written as 3.58.

What next?

Hopefully, you are getting much better at solving equations. If you want more practice at solving equations with decimal solutions, you can make up your own. Just write down an expression and put it equal to any number you choose. Then try to solve it. To check whether you are right, use substitution.

Try it yourself!

1. **Expand the brackets** of these equations first.

   Then **solve** each equation, using either the **balancing** or the **inverses** method. Do your working out *on paper*.

   $5(a + 2) = 30$ $3(b + 4) = 15$ $2(c − 5) = 6$

   $5a + 10 = 30$

   $a = $ _____

   $4(h − 3) = 28$ $9(j + 1) = 36$ $2(3k − 5) = 32$

   $5(2m − 6) = 30$ $32 = 2(5n + 6)$ $15 = 3(4p − 7)$

   Remember to check all solutions by **substituting**.

2. **Solve** these **equations** using whichever method you choose.

   These equations have **decimal** solutions.
   Do your working out *on paper*. Use a calculator.

   $4e + 8 = 18$ $10 = 12f + 1$ $2 = 5g − 4$

   $2(h − 3) = 7$ $4(j + 8) = 58$ $5(2k − 1) = 38$

   $3m − 6 = 41$ $7(n + 4) = 53$ $6(3p − 7) = 55$

   Remember to check all solutions by **substituting**.

Letters on both sides of an equation

Practice

- Some equations have a letter on both sides, like this:

$$5y - 1 = 3y + 4$$

To **solve equations** like these, use **balancing** to get the letters all on one side first.

- So, with our example, to get all the y's on one side of the equation (it does not matter which side) *add or subtract the same number of y's from both sides.*

$$5y - 1 = 3y + 4$$
$$-3y \qquad -3y$$
$$2y - 1 = 4$$

To get rid of **3y** from the right, **subtract 3y** from both sides.

- This is a new equation with the letter y on one side only. This new **equivalent** equation can be solved in the same way as before, using either the **balancing** or **inverses** method.

balancing

$$2y - 1 = 4$$
$$+ 1 \qquad + 1$$
$$2y = 5$$
$$\div 2 \qquad \div 2$$
$$y = 2.5$$

inverses

$$2y - 1 = 4$$

Start with y → multiply by 2 → subtract 1 → to get to 4
to get to y ← divide by 2 ← add 1 ← Start with 4

$(4 + 1) \div 2 = y$
$5 \div 2 = y$
so $y = 2.5$

- As always, check the solution by **substituting** the number for the letter on one side to see if it equals what is on the other side.

$$5y - 1 = 3y + 4 \qquad y = 2.5$$

$5 \times 2.5 - 1$ should equal $3 \times 2.5 + 4$
$12.5 - 1 = 11.5 \qquad 7.5 + 4 = 11.5$

They are both equal, so $y = 2.5$ is correct.

Clues and tips
Remind yourself about the **balancing** methods by looking again at pages 21 and 22. Make sure you read THE RULES.

Remember this
Remember that when adding and subtracting parts of an expression (see page 7) only add or subtract a **number** from a **number** or a **letter** from the same **letter**. Like this:

$5a - 5 + 2a$
$= 7a - 5$

$4b + 8 - 4b = 8$

Watch out
The new equation is **equivalent** to (worth the same as) the original one, so it will have the same solution (and it is much easier to solve).

Remember this
Notice that the solution is substituted into the *original* equation.

Clues and tips

For the second part of question 1, if you are not sure whether to subtract $3b$ or $5b$, always subtract the *smaller* number of b's.

A common mistake

A common mistake that people make is to forget to write the letter after a subtraction.

$6a - 4a = 2a$

This is RIGHT

Think of it as '6 lots of a' subtract '4 lots of a' equals '2 lots of a'.

It is WRONG to write

$6a - 4a = 2$

Use a calculator if the division is too hard to do in your head. Round your answers if necessary.

Watch out for the last three equations of question 2. To get rid of $-2k$ from one side you will need to add $2k$.

What next?

If you are stuck getting a new equation with letters on one side only, look again at pages 9 and 10.

Try it yourself!

1. **Solve** these **equations** by first getting the letters on one side.

   Check all solutions by **substituting** into the original equation.

   $4a + 8 = 6a - 2$ $5b - 4 = 3b + 6$

   $-4a -4a$
   $8 = 2a - 2$

   (Now solve $8 = 2a - 2$)

   $8c + 1 = 9c - 4$ $6d - 3 = 2d + 7$

   $10e - 6 = 4e + 9$ $3f - 4 = 6f - 12$

2. **Solve** these **equations**. Do your working out *on paper*.

   $4g + 1 = 3g + 8$ $5h - 5 = 3h + 2$ $7j - 1 = 4j + 6$

   $6k + 4 = 20 - 2k$ $4n - 8 = 10 - 5n$ $2p + 4 = 34 - 6p$

   Remember to check all solutions by **substituting**.

Formulae

Practice

- Algebra is used for many different purposes in real life. One of the most important is being able to **substitute** values into a **formula**.

$$A = \tfrac{1}{2}bh \qquad n = (x + y) \div 2 \qquad F = ma$$

$$A = \tfrac{1}{2}(a + b)h \qquad F = \frac{9C}{5} + 32 \qquad v = u + at$$

- A formula shows the relationship between two or more things. **Formulae** are like **equations**: they have an equals sign. The first formula above tells us the relationship between the **area** of a triangle (A) and its **base** (b) and **height** (h).

$$A = \tfrac{1}{2}bh$$

If the base and height are known, the area can be worked out.

- These are worked out by substituting (see pages 11 and 12 for a reminder).

  Here, it is said that **A** is the **subject of the formula**. It is alone on one side of the equals sign.

  Find the area of a triangle where $b = 4$ cm and $h = 9$ cm.

  $$A = \tfrac{1}{2}bh$$

  $A = \tfrac{1}{2} \times 4 \times 9 =$ **18 cm²**

- The second formula above shows how to find a number (n) that is halfway between two other numbers (x and y). **n** is the subject of the formula.

  It is possible to make any letter in a formula the subject of the formula. The same balancing rules as before are used. (See pages 21 and 22.)

  Find the number that is halfway between 28 and 54.

  $$n = (x + y) \div 2$$

  $n = (28 + 54) \div 2 =$ **41**

- Making x the subject of the formula:

$$n = (x + y) \div 2$$

Let us get rid of the **÷ 2** on the right by multiplying both sides by 2.

To get rid of the **+ y** on the right, subtract y from both sides.

×2   ×2
2n = x + y
−y   −y
2n − y = x

This gives **2n − y = x** or **x = 2n − y**

Word wise
The plural of **formula** is **formulae**.

Remember this
Remember that the multiplication sign is not usually used in algebra, the numbers or letters are just written next to each other.

$F = m \times a$ is the same as $F = ma$.

This formula is used in science to show the relationship between force, mass and acceleration.

Why change the subject?
Look at the formula for the area of a triangle:

$$A = \tfrac{1}{2}bh$$

Now, suppose you are given the **area** and the **base**, could you work out the **height**? To do so, you would need to change the **subject of the formula** to get the formula:

$$h = 2A \div b$$

Then it is easy.

More confident in algebra now?

Tick the following topics you feel confident with:

Expressions
- Simplifying expressions (pages 3–4) ☐
- Collecting like terms (pages 5–6) ☐
- Adding and subtracting letters (pages 7–8) ☐
- Constants and variables (pages 9–10) ☐
- Substitution (pages 11–12) ☐
- Expanding brackets and factorising (pages 13–14) ☐

Equations
- Solving simple equations (pages 19–20) ☐
- Solving equations by balancing (pages 21–22) ☐
- Solving equations using inverses (pages 23–24) ☐
- Solving more complex equations (pages 25–26) ☐
- Letters on both sides of an equation (pages 27–28) ☐
- Formulae (pages 29–30) ☐

Read through any pages again to make sure you understand.

Try it yourself!

1. **Substitute** the values shown into the following formulae. Do your working out *on paper*.

   $$A = \tfrac{1}{2} bh$$ Find the area of a triangle (A) if:

   $b = 5$ cm and $h = 3$ cm $\quad$ $b = 9$ cm and $h = 4$ cm

   $b = 3$ cm and $h = 10$ cm $\quad$ $b = 8$ cm and $h = 5$ cm

   $$n = (x + y) \div 2$$ Find the number (n) that lies halfway between:

   $x = 32, y = 48$ $\quad$ $x = 17, y = 45$

   $$A = \tfrac{1}{2}(a + b)h$$ Find the area of a trapezium (A) if:

   $a = 3$ cm, $b = 5$ cm and $h = 3$ cm $\quad$ $a = 2$ cm, $b = 8$ cm and $h = 4$ cm

   $$F = \frac{9C}{5} + 32$$ Find the temperature in Fahrenheit (F) if:

   $C = 10$ degrees Celsius $\quad$ $C = 15$ degrees Celsius

2. Working out *on paper*, make d the **subject of each formula**.

   $$C = 7d + 50 \qquad C = 4d + 12$$

   $\quad -50 \qquad\qquad -50$
   $C - 50 = 7d$
   $\quad \div 7 \quad \div 7$
   $(C - 50) \div 7 = d$

   $$C = 3d - 15 \qquad C = 5d - 4$$

3. Find d in each formula above if $C = 100$.

Answers

SIMPLIFYING EXPRESSIONS (PAGE 4)
1. $5a$ $6a$ $5a$ $8a$ $7a$ $11a$ $12a$ $15a$
2. true   true   true   false   false   false   true   true   false   false
3. $5m$ $8g$ $7p$ $7s$ $9c$ $16d$ $13y$ $15k$

COLLECTING LIKE TERMS (PAGE 6)
1. $4a + 6b$ (or $6b + 4a$)
   $4a + 2b$ (or $2b + 4a$)
   $2a + 3b$ (or $3b + 2a$)
   $2a + 6b$ (or $6b + 2a$)
   $4a + 3b$ (or $3b + 4a$)
   $8a + 3b$ (or $3b + 8a$)
2. $4a + 3b$ ✓
   $4a + 3b$ ✓
   $6a + b$
   $4a + 3b$ ✓
   $4a + 3b$ ✓
   $4a + 3b$ ✓
3. $4g + 2h$ (or $2h + 4g$)
   $5m + 3n$ (or $3n + 5m$)
   $7c + 3d$ (or $3d + 7c$)
   $13e + 3f$ (or $3f + 13e$)
   $6x + 7y$ (or $7y + 6x$)
   $9j + 6k$ (or $6k + 9j$)
4. $9a + 3b + 4c$ (or these in any order)
   $4p + 9q + 3r$ (or these in any order)
   $11x + 8y + 8z$ (or these in any order)

ADDING AND SUBTRACTING LETTERS (PAGE 8)
1. $4a$
   $4a$
   $6a$
   $3a + 5b$ (or $5b + 3a$)
   $2a + 5b$ (or $5b + 2a$)
   $4a + 4b$ (or $4b + 4a$)
   $5a + b$ (or $b + 5a$)
   $4b$
   $3a + 6b$ (or $6b + 3a$)
   $6a + b$ (or $b + 6a$)
   $a + b$ (or $b + a$)
   $6a$
2. $3a + 7b$ (or $7b + 3a$)
   $5a + 5b$ (or $5b + 5a$)
   $3a + 3b$ (or $3b + 3a$)
   $3a$
3. $2a - 2b$ (or $-2b + 2a$)
   $4a - 6b$ (or $-6b + 4a$)
   $-a + 3b$ (or $3b - a$)
   $-3a + 6b$ (or $6b - 3a$)
   $-a + 3b$ (or $3b - a$)
   $a - 5b$ (or $-5b + a$)

CONSTANTS AND VARIABLES (PAGE 10)
1. $6a + 10b + 7$ (or these in any order)
   $9a + 11b + 3$ (or these in any order)
   $11a + 6b - 2$ (or these in any order)
   $7a + 8b + 3$ (or these in any order)
   $7a + 4b + 9$ (or these in any order)
2. $5a + 7b + 6$ (or these in any order)
   $a + 7b + 1$ (or these in any order)
   $7a - 3$ (or these in any order)
   $3a + 2b - 4$ (or these in any order)
3. $2c + 3d + 4$ (or these in any order)
   $8m - n + 3$ (or these in any order)
   $3g + h$ (or these in any order)
   $s + 10t$ (or these in any order)

SUBSTITUTION (PAGE 11)
£23   £29   £54   £22

SUBSTITUTION (PAGE 12)
1. $5a = 20$ $7y = 14$ $8d = 40$ $6k + 1 = 67$
   $9x + 5 = 95$ $5g + 4 = 19$ $10q - 2 = 8$
2. 26   16   13   18
3. 50   41   25   24   100   29   88   18

EXPANDING BRACKETS AND FACTORISING (PAGE 14)
1. $2a + 2b$
   $4y - 8$
   $5c + 10$
   $3k + 18$
   $6m + 6n$
   $14a - 7$
   $20g + 4h$
   $12f - 6e$
   $80s + 24t$
   $15y - 35$
   $3a + 9b - 6$
   $2m + 14n + 8$
   $20c + 5d - 15e$
   $6g - 12h - 30$
2. $2(a + b)$
   $2(c - 2)$
   $5(d + 2)$
   $3(k + 2)$
   $2(3m + 2n)$
   $2(a - 6)$
   $10(g + 2h)$
   $2(3f - e)$
   $3(5s + t)$
   $5(y - 5)$
   $2(a + 2b - 3)$
   $2(m + 3n + 2)$

Answers

$5(3c + d - 2e)$
$4(2g - h - 3)$

SOLVING SIMPLE EQUATIONS (PAGE 20)

1. $a = 3$
$b = 8$
$c = 8$
$d = 3$
$e = 2$
$f = 18$
$g = 10$
$h = 5$
$j = 2$
$k = 4$
$m = 6$
$n = 7$

2. $n + 6 = 23, n = 17$
$n - 11 = 44, n = 55$
$27 - n = 18, n = 9$
$5n = 40, n = 8$

3. $p = 20$
$q = 20$
$r = 9$
$s = 5$
$t = 40$
$u = 48$

SOLVING EQUATIONS BY BALANCING (PAGE 22)

1. $b = 10$
$c = 8$
$d = 7$
$e = 6$

2. $f = 11$
$g = 4$
$h = 5$
$k = 3$

SOLVING EQUATIONS USING INVERSES (PAGE 24)

1. $b = 10$
$c = 8$
$d = 7$

2. $e = 5$
$f = 8$
$g = 5$
$h = 5$
$j = 9$
$k = 11$
$m = 6$
$n = 7$
$p = 8$

SOLVING MORE COMPLEX EQUATIONS (PAGE 26)

1. $5a + 10 = 30; a = 4$
$3b + 12 = 15; b = 1$
$2c - 10 = 6; c = 8$
$4h - 12 = 28; h = 10$
$9j + 9 = 36; j = 3$
$6k - 10 = 32; k = 7$
$10m - 30 = 30; m = 6$
$32 = 10n + 12; n = 2$
$15 = 12p - 21; p = 3$

2. $e = 2.5$
$f = 0.75$
$g = 1.2$
$h = 6.5$
$j = 6.5$
$k = 4.3$
$m = 15.67$
$n = 3.57$
$p = 5.39$

LETTERS ON BOTH SIDES OF AN EQUATION (PAGE 28)

1. $a = 5$
$b = 5$
$c = 5$
$d = 2.5$
$e = 2.5$
$f = 2.67$

2. $g = 7$
$h = 3.5$
$j = 2.33$
$k = 2$
$n = 2$
$p = 3.75$

FORMULAE (PAGE 30)

1. 7.5 cm^2 18 cm^2 15 cm^2 20 cm^2
40 31 12 cm^2 20 cm^2
50 °F 59 °F

2. $(C - 50) \div 7 = d$
$(C - 12) \div 4 = d$
$(C + 15) \div 3 = d$
$(C + 4) \div 5 = d$

3. $d = 7.14$
$d = 22$
$d = 38.33$
$d = 20.8$